Spring Boot Intermediate Microservices

Resilient Microservices with Spring Boot 2 and Spring Cloud

Jens Boje

CODEBOJE
Brief books for developers

Spring Boot Intermediate Microservices
Jens Boje

Published in 2017 by Jens Boje

Jens Boje
Pfungststr. 3
60314 Frankfurt
Germany

On the web: *http://codeboje.de*
Please send errors to *book@codeboje.de*

Publisher: Jens Boje
Illustraion on Cover: Created by Dooder - Freepik.com

Contents

Introduction

This book's approach differs from that of other programming books that you may have encountered. That's because I believe that the best way to learn a new framework or language is to build applications using it.

We will build upon our sample microservice we created in the book "Spring Boot - How to get Started and Build a Microservice", add a consuming application and then build a fault tolerant environment using common microservice patterns.

What we will build in this book

- We start with a simple consuming application using Springs RestTemplate to access the microservice

- We enhance this by adding Spring Retry for making it a bit more reliable

- We add client-side load balancing to make it even more reliable

- We then replace our retry mechanism with the circuit breaker pattern to level up

- We introduce service discovery patterns to make it easier to add new instances of a microservice

- We introduce a gateway to make the UI of the consumer and the API of the commentstore microservice available behind one entry point

- As the services and thus complexity grow we will externalize the configuration

The full source code for this book's sample applications is available on GitHub: Link (https://github.com/azarai/spring-boot-intermediate-microservices)

Each step resides in its own branch.

I'll explain the most relevant code in the book with code samples. However, I do skip the code for certain simple helper classes, but you can always find them in the source code.

What You Will Need

- Java 8

- Maven (3.2+)

- Text editor or IDE of your choice. I use Spring Tools Suite but it is not required to follow along.

Installing and setting them up is not in the scope of this book.

Building the Consumer Application

The consumer application is a simple Spring Boot application with one page displaying a mock product, showing the comments for it, and a form to submit a new comment. The product and product retrieval are mocked; the comments are actually handled. In a real application, the products would be in its own microservice and the same principals apply as we are using with the commentstore microservice.

You can find the source code in the GitHub repository in the branch *consumer-simple*.

I recommend that you clone the repository and begin with the master branch, and gradually follow along. The master branch already contains an updated version of the commentstore microservice using Spring Boot 2. I also deployed it to Heroku and for the first few steps, you can use my Heroku instance as the backend. However, starting with the service registry you will need to run all locally.

The commentstore is deployed at:
https://boiling-retreat-23464.herokuapp.com

Let's start with implementing the consumer application.

Create a new Spring Boot application using the *web, thymeleaf, devtools* and *test* starters. Your pom should look like:

```
<project
  xmlns="http://maven.apache.org/POM/4.0.0"
  xmlns:xsi="http://www.w3.org/2001/XMLSchema-instance"
```

```xml
    xsi:schemaLocation="http://maven.apache.org/POM/4.0.0
        http://maven.apache.org/xsd/maven-4.0.0.xsd">
    <modelVersion>4.0.0</modelVersion>
    <parent>
        <groupId>org.springframework.boot</groupId>
        <artifactId>spring-boot-starter-parent</artifactId>
        <version>2.0.0.M2</version>
    </parent>
    <groupId>de.codeboje.springbootbook</groupId>
    <version>1.0.0-SNAPSHOT</version>
    <artifactId>consumer</artifactId>
    <name>Spring Boot Intermediate Microservice Book -
Consumer App</name>

    <dependencies>
        <dependency>
            <groupId>org.springframework.boot</groupId>
            <artifactId>spring-boot-starter-web</artifactId>
        </dependency>
        <dependency>
            <groupId>org.springframework.boot</groupId>
            <artifactId>spring-boot-starter-thymeleaf</
artifactId>
        </dependency>
        <dependency>
            <groupId>org.springframework.boot</groupId>
            <artifactId>spring-boot-devtools</artifactId>
            <optional>true</optional>
        </dependency>
        <dependency>
            <groupId>org.springframework.boot</groupId>
            <artifactId>spring-boot-starter-test</artifactId>
            <scope>test</scope>
        </dependency>
    </dependencies>
</project>
```

Next, we will add the commentstore commons module which contains the DTO used in our API and a *ObjectMapper*, so we use the same rules on each side.

```
<dependency>
  <groupId>de.codeboje.springbootbook</groupId>
  <artifactId>commons</artifactId>
  <version>1.0.0-SNAPSHOT</version>
</dependency>
```

This module is part of the commentstore application, so clone the git repository and run a

```
mvn clean install
```

in the root dir.

Create the *ConsumerApplication* as with any other SpringBoot application.

```
@SpringBootApplication
public class ConsumerApplication {

    public static void main(String[] args)
      throws Exception {
        SpringApplication.run(
          ConsumerApplication.class, args
        );
    }

}
```

Next, we'll add our *CommentstoreObjectMapper* and mark it as the primary bean for the *ObjectMapper*. Each *@Component* in the Spring Context requesting a *ObjectMapper* will now receive ours — even when multiple should be available.

```
@Bean
@Primary
ObjectMapper objectMapper() {
    return new CommentstoreObjectMapper();
}
```

Now we can start with the interesting things. For accessing the microservice, we are using the *RestTemplate* which is part of Spring Web and provides a generic way for working with Rest APIs. The benefit it offers is that you work with your data classes with Spring handling the transformations to and from various formats, i.e. JSON, GSON, XML, etc.

Before we can use it, we must set up a bean first.

```
@Bean
RestTemplate restTemplate(
  @Value("${commentstore.auth.user}")
  String username,
  @Value("${commentstore.auth.password}")
  String password,
  RestTemplateBuilder restTemplateBuilder)
{
    RestTemplate restTemplate =
                        restTemplateBuilder.build();
    restTemplate.getInterceptors().add(
      0,
      new BasicAuthorizationInterceptor(
        username,
        password
      )
    );
    return restTemplate;
}
```

The commentstore API is protected by Basic auth using *admin* and *mypassword* as the credentials so we inject the credentials using the *@Value* annotation. Spring will scan the environment for these. We are providing the values in the *application.properties* file.

```
commentstore.auth.user=admin
commentstore.auth.password=mypassword
```

RestTemplateBuilder is a helper class for setting up a *RestTemplate* and is especially useful when testing later with a mock. We don't do any specialty; we just call the *build* method.

Next, we add the *BasicAuthorizationInterceptor* for handling Basic authentication. It only needs the username and password from us and is automatically used on each request.

Now the *RestTemplate* is ready to use for our service class.

Create *CommentService*, inject the endpoint of our commentstore (using the same mechanism as before) and the *RestTemplate*.

```
@Service
public class CommentService {

    @Value("${commentstore.endpoint}")
    private String endpoint;

    @Autowired
    private RestTemplate restTemplate;
}
```

For making it available in the Spring Context, add it to the *ConsumerApplication*:

```
@Bean
CommentService commentService() {
    return new CommentService();
}
```

And last, but not least, we declare the *commentstore.endpoint* in the *application.properties* file:

```
commentstore.endpoint=https://boiling-
retreat-23464.herokuapp.com
```

Now we will start with retrieving the comments for a given product using the *RestTemplate*.

```
public CommentDTO[] getComments(String productId) {
    CommentDTO[] response = restTemplate.getForObject(
      endpoint + "/list/" + productId,
      new CommentDTO[0].getClass()
    );

    return response;
}
```

getForObject will make a GET request to the given endpoint and will try to convert whatever will come back to the class given. As the *list* returns a list of *CommentDTO* we will pass a *CommentDTO* array as the type of the response. In our case, the JSON converter will try to convert the resulting JSON into this object type. There's no way with, at least with the convenience methods, to define the result type as something like *List<CommentDTO>*, but you can use the array type and then convert it to a list using *Arrasy.asList*. You can, however, use the central *exchange* method, which all the convenience methods use internally anyway, and use a *Parameterized-TypeReference* like:

```
ResponseEntity<List<CommentDTO>> responseEntity =
  restTemplate.exchange(
    endpoint + "/list/" + productId,
    HttpMethod.GET,
    null,
    new ParameterizedTypeReference<List<CommentDTO>>() {}
  );
responseEntity.getBody(); // gets the List
```

When you need access to the status code or HTTP headers, you can use the *getForEntity* method which returns a *ResponseEntity* containing this information plus the converted object.

PUT, DELETE, and POST do have their own convenience methods which essentially behave the same. If the commentstore endpoint would handle a JSON for POST, we could just do the same with *postForObject*. However, posting new comments to the commentstore is done *form-urlencoded*. We can also do that with the *RestTemplate*.

postForEntity provides a method signature for custom defining the request. We'll use this and set up a *HttpEntity* as a *form-urlencoded* request and set the values manually:

```java
public String postComment(CommentForm comment) {
    HttpHeaders headers = new HttpHeaders();
    headers.setContentType(
            MediaType.APPLICATION_FORM_URLENCODED
    );

    MultiValueMap<String, String> map= new
                LinkedMultiValueMap<String, String>();
    map.add("emailAddress", comment.getEmailAddress());
    map.add("comment", comment.getComment());
    map.add("pageId", comment.getProductId());
    map.add("username", comment.getUsername());

    HttpEntity<MultiValueMap<String, String>> request =
      new HttpEntity<MultiValueMap<String, String>>(
          map, headers
      );

    ResponseEntity<String> response =
    restTemplate.postForEntity(
      endpoint + "/create/",
      request,
      String.class
    );

    return response.getBody();
}
```

CommentForm is a simple POJO with some fields and is used in the UI and service.

```java
public class CommentForm {
    private String productId;
    private String username;
    private String emailAddress;
    private String comment;

    //getter and setter omitted
}
```

Before we continue with the consumer application, we will write a test for the *CommentService*.

Testing

Create the *ConsumerServiceTest* test and set it up as a Spring test. Inject the *CommentService, ObjectMapper* and *endpoint*.

```java
@RunWith(SpringRunner.class)
@RestClientTest(CommentService.class)
public class ConsumerServiceTest {

    @Value("${commentstore.endpoint}")
    private String endpoint;

    @Autowired
    private CommentService commentService;

    @Autowired
    private MockRestServiceServer server;

    @Autowired
    private ObjectMapper objectMapper;
}
```

@RestClientTest is a custom annotation for mocking rest clients using the *RestTemplate* and requires the *RestTemplate* to be set up by the *RestTemplateBuilder*. It will provide a *MockRestServiceServer* we can use to mock server responses.

```
@Test
public void whenGetComments_thenReturnEmpty() {

    final String productId = "product4712";
    server.expect(
            requestTo(
                endpoint + "/list/" + productId
            )
    )
    .andRespond(
            withSuccess(
                "[]",
                MediaType.APPLICATION_JSON
            )
    );

    CommentDTO[] comments = commentService
                            .getComments(productId);

    assertEquals(0, comments.length);

    server.verify();
}
```

MockRestServiceServer uses a Fluent API in a similar style like Mockito and the other Spring test support. Read it as the mock server expects a request being made to *endpoint* + *"/list/"* + *productId* and it will respond successfully with an empty JSON array.

We'll retrieve the comments from the *CommentService*, verify that it is empty, and also confirm that the request was actually made (*server.verify()*).

You can test now the get method, but with a nonempty response as an exercise. A solution is in the source code. Hint: You can use the injected *ObjectMapper* to return a valid JSON.

The UI

The UI consists of a single *Controller* and a Thymeleaf template to display a product and its comments.

Create *ProductController,* mark it as a Spring MVC *@Controller,* and inject the *CommentService.*

```
@Controller
public class ProductController {

    @Autowired
    private CommentService commentService;
}
```

For a real application, we would have an own service for handling product. But in the sample, we are going to simply hard mock it here.

Create the simple POJO *Product* as an inner class like:

```
class Product {
    private String id;
    private String title;
    private String description;

    //getter and setter omitted
}
```

And provide a method for creating a dummy instance:

```
private Product getDummyProduct() {
    final Product p = new Product();
    p.setId("product4711");
    p.setTitle("Product 4711 - Title");
    p.setDescription("Product 4711 is the greatest
                        product in the world.");
    return p;
}
```

Next, we define an endpoint on the root path, which will create the dummy product, and retrieve the comments and forwards to a template, all using plain regular Spring MVC.

```
@RequestMapping("/")
public String home(Model model) {
    final Product product = getDummyProduct();

    final CommentDTO[] comments = commentService.
                        getComments(product.getId());

    model.addAttribute("product", product);
    model.addAttribute("comments", comments);
    model.addAttribute("newcomment", new CommentForm());
    return "index";
}
```

The attributes we set on the model are then accessible in the template:

- product: the product instance

- comments: the list of all comments for the product

- newcomment: an instance for adding a new comment via a form

Next, create the *index.html* template in *src/main_resources/templates*. Use the file from the repository as a reference or just copy it as I am only covering the essentials here.

Display our product:

```
<div class="col-6">
    <h1 th:text="${product.title}"></h1>
    <p th:text="${product.id}" />
    <p class="lead" th:text="${product.description}" />
</div>
```

Display all comments:

```
<th:block th:each="comment: ${comments}">
    <div class="row">
        <div class="col">
            <h5 th:text="'by ' + ${comment.username}"></h5>
            <p th:text="${comment.created}"></p>
            <p>
                <span th:text="${comment.comment}"></span>
            </p>
            <hr>
        </div>
    </div>
</th:block>
```

The form for adding a new comment is:

```
<form action="#" th:action="@{/postComment}"
    th:object="${newcomment}" method="post">
    <input type="hidden" th:name="productId"
     th:value="${product.id}" />
    <p>
        Name: <input type="text" th:field="*{username}"
            required="required" />
    </p>
    <p>
        Email: <input type="email"
                th:field="*{emailAddress}"
                required="required" />
    </p>
    <p>
        Comment: <input type="text"
```

```
            th:field="*{comment}"
            required="required" />
    </p>
    <p>
        <input type="submit" value="Submit" />
        <input type=„reset" value="Reset" />
    </p>
</form>
```

We use plain Thymeleaf here.

So, when you start the application now and access *http://localhost: 8080/* you should get a nice page with the product details and no comments on it.

What's left is to add the handling of the form post in the *Product-Controller*. Add:

```
@PostMapping("/postComment")
public String commentSubmit(@ModelAttribute CommentForm
comment) {
    commentService.postComment(comment);
    return "redirect:/";
}
```

When hitting the submit button, the form is posted to */postComment* with the fields and due *@ModelAttribute CommentForm* automatically mapped to a *CommentForm* by Spring MVC. We then use the *CommentService* to post the comment to the commentstore microservice and redirect back to the root path. In the end, you should see the product details again with your comment on it, too.

Now that we have implemented it, we will discuss how reliable it is.

Conclusion

Accessing a remote service with the *RestTemplate* is pretty straight forward. However, in this simple case, it does have some real drawbacks. Let's take a closer look.

What would happen if our commentstore microservice was down?

The request to it would fail and as it is now, the whole product display would fail. Meaning no commentstore, no product front-end. That's bad for a production site.

You can, of course, surround the comment retrieval with a try-catch block and in the case of an error just return a useful result. Maybe an empty list, or perhaps a cached version of the comments.

The product details would work again — despite the commentstore being offline. But, you can't post any comment. If the customer was in the middle of posting a comment and the commentstore went down, or was unresponsive for a second, the post would fail. Sure, you can redirect the customer again to the page with the comment form still filled out. But, if it happens too frequently, they'll leave.

The classic way to tackle this problem is to add a server side load balancer in front of the commentstore and host at least two instances of it. This works, but depending on the number of services involved in a scenario, it can become quite complex and costly. You have to have at least 3 servers per service, one for the load balancer, and two for the actual service. This setup is usually configured manually and fixed, i.e. when adding a new service you'll need to add it to a configuration file and maybe even restart the load balancer. In addition, the load balancer usually is part of the infrastructure and in a corporate world handled by a different team with different priorities, etc. Fixing something fast can be a nightmare.

Imagine a service with 3 instances and they all go down at the same time and though an essential part of the whole application is unavailable. There is no chance of getting a fourth rescue server up quickly behind the load balancer. And, the services won't start up. That's no fun; it's happened to me as I was on duty.

Here's another scenario: The application experiences an unusually high load and the services slow down or die. When one dies, the others receive the requests and eventually die too. I am exaggerating a bit, but nonetheless, it is a common problem. One could keep backup servers in spare and just turn them on. However, many companies don't want the costs incurred with this version, and depending on the company, it might take weeks or months till a new server is ready.

The microservice architecture has solutions to some of these problems, and in combination with cloud hosting, one can also solve the problem of keeping spare servers on hold. In the next chapters, we'll explore solutions to these problems and improve our sample step by step.

We will begin with adding some retry functionality in the next chapter.

Recap

Before we move on to the next variant, let's check you understanding with some open-ended questions.

- How do you set up basic auth in the RestTemplate?

- How can you test a service using the RestTemplate?

- Are there any prerequisites for using the @RestClientTest?

- How reliable is the simple version with the RestTemplate?

Basic Retry and Fallback Functionality

We discussed in the last chapter, that our first simple approach has some disadvantages. Starting with this chapter, we are going to improve it step-by-step. The first one we are going to change is that we will retry a failed request. So, when a call to the commentstore failed, we assume it might only be a temporary problem and just retry the request.

You can find the working sample in the branch *consumer-retry*.

Spring Retry is a library for providing a common set of functionality for retrying something. It is not limited to *RestTemplate* and can be easily used outside of Spring too. However, we are going to use the annotation-driven way and highly integrate with Spring.

To get started, add the following dependencies to the pom:

```
<dependency>
  <groupId>org.springframework.retry</groupId>
  <artifactId>spring-retry</artifactId>
</dependency>
<dependency>
  <groupId>org.springframework.boot</groupId>
  <artifactId>spring-boot-starter-aop</artifactId>
</dependency>
```

The first is Spring Retry and the second is needed to use the annotation variation. Spring Retry uses aspects here and wraps a retryable class with a proxy.

For enabling the annotation processing, we must add the *@EnableRetry* to *ConsumerApplication* like:

```
@SpringBootApplication
@EnableRetry
public class ConsumerApplication {
    //omitted
}
```

Spring Retry will now look for methods annotated with *@Retryable* and *@Recover*. A method annotated with *@Retryable* will be called again in case of an Exception following some rules. More on that in a minute. And a method annotated with *@Recover* is called when the retries for a particular method failed.

Let's first configure it for our *CommentService* and then we take a look at the rules involved. Add it to the *getComments* like:

```
@Retryable
public CommentDTO[] getComments(String productId) {
    // ommitted
}
```

When we only add the annotation but do not configure any parameter, Spring Retry will use some defaults. Any *Exception* thrown will trigger a retry and it tries for a max of three attempts. It does also wait for a second between each try.

In the case of a failed *getComments* it would retry a request three times which might be too much for displaying our product. So let's reduce it to just one try:

```
@Retryable(maxAttempts=1)
public CommentDTO[] getComments(String productId) {
    // omitted
}
```

Start the consumer application but turn the commentstore off. You should see in the logs that the request is sent just once. Adjust *maxAttempts* to another value and note that it repeats the request now. However, it will still fail the whole product details in the end. But we can define a fallback with *@Recover* which is called when all retries failed. It is possible to have more than one method annotated with *@Recover* in a class and Spring Retry follows some rules to determine the fallback method.

First, the retry and recovery method must be in the same class. Second, they must have the same return value. The recovery method can either have no parameters at all ,or you can use some optionally arguments provided by Spring Retry: the *Exception* thrown and a list (or partial list) of the parameters of the retryable method in the same order.

Adding one for *getComments* could look like:

```
@Recover
public CommentDTO[] recover(Throwable e, String
productId) {
    LOGGER.info("requesting comments for product {}
failed, retries exceeded", productId);
    return new CommentDTO[0];
}
```

In the example, we just log it and return an empty array, so the product details work but no comments are shown. However, you are not limited by that and you may handle it in a way that makes sense for a particular problem.

When a user posts a new comment and the request to the commentstore fails, we should extend the retries a bit. Therefore, extend the retries to 5 attempts using *maxAttempts* and also increase the delay between each try to 2 seconds by declaring a backoff policy (*@Backoff*).

```
@Retryable(
  maxAttempts=5,
  backoff=@Backoff(delay=2000)
)
public String postComment(CommentForm comment) {
    // omitted
}
```

We use a simple backoff which is a fixed time and always the same between two tries, but Spring Retry supports much more like exponential delays and max times, etc. Check out the documentation (https://github.com/spring-projects/spring-retry) for its full capabilities.

What's left is handling the failed retries. I think it is a good exercise for you to add the recovery method. I'll wait here and when you are done, we can discuss how we improved it.

Conclusion

The initial version of our application was not reliable in any forms. When the commentstore has a hickup or plainly dies, the consumer application would share the same fate. It would be, de facto, dead as well.

By adding retry and fallback strategies using Spring Retry, we changed it favorably and kept the consumer application alive, even when the commentstore died. We did this by simply adding a fallback method for each request. When a customer now views the product details, he will receive them regardless of the state of the commentstore.

However, when the customer tries to post a comment, it would still fail. By adding retry capabilities to the request, we could at least cover some hickups and load problems in the commentstore. If the commentstore is slow and the first request fails, we just try it a couple of times again and either succeed or fail. It still won't protect us from complete outages of the commentstore. For that, we are going to add a second instance of it and will use a technique called client-side load balancing in the next chapter.

Recap

Before we move on to the next variant, let's check your understanding with some open-ended questions:

- How do you set up Spring Retry support?

- Can you use Spring Retry without Spring?

- Does it compare to the previous simple version?

- Did we make anything better regarding the reliability of the application?

Client-Side Load Balancing

In the last chapter, we added some basic retry and fallback functionality and discussed how it improved our application. Now, we are going to add a second instance of the microservice and use a client-side load balancing strategy to make it more reliable.

We are using Spring Cloud for this or more concrete, the Ribbon client. The Ribbon client is basically a proxy around a *RestTemplate* and uses the Netflix OSS library internally to provide client-side load balancing.

The example is in the branch *consumer-client-loadbalancing-retry*.

To get started, add the following dependency to the pom:

```
<dependency>
  <groupId>org.springframework.cloud</groupId>
  <artifactId>spring-cloud-starter-ribbon</artifactId>
</dependency>
```

To enable the Ribbon client, we add the *@RibbonClient* annotation to our *ConsumerApplication* or any other @Configuration_ annotated class.

```
@SpringBootApplication
@EnableRetry
@RibbonClient(
  name = "commentstore",
  configuration = RibbonConfig.class
)
public class ConsumerApplication {
    //omitted code
}
```

name is a unique identifier of the Ribbon client and we will use it in the requesting URLs later. You can pass additional configuration with the *configuration* parameter like ping checks, availability rules, etc. If you do not provide a *configuration* it will use the defaults from the *RibbonClientConfiguration*.

However, we are overriding two defaults by defining the *@Bean* again.

```
public class RibbonConfig {

    @Autowired
    IClientConfig ribbonClientConfig;

    @Bean
    public IPing ribbonPing(IClientConfig config) {
        return new PingUrl(true, "/application/info");
    }

    @Bean
    public IRule ribbonRule(IClientConfig config) {
        return new AvailabilityFilteringRule();
    }
}
```

First, we define that the Ribbon client should actually ping our service to determine if it is available or not by using the *PingUrl* class. Its first parameter defines if the ping URL is secure (aka https) and if you are using my Heroku deployed commentstore, keep it at true. However, if you run the commentstore locally, change it to *false*. The second parameter is the URL to ping at the server. It's best to use some kind of health check endpoint. For the test, the info endpoint automatically provided by the SpringBoot actuators is enough.

Second, we will use a *AvailabilityFilteringRule* which filters the servers by availability. The Ribbon client uses a RoundRobin strategy for picking the next server, i.e. on each request, it simply picks the next server in the list and at the end of the list, just starts at the beginning again. The provided *IRule* implementations enhance this a bit by determining which server to pick. The *AvailabilityFilteringRule* filters out an unresponsive server, either by circuit break trips, missed pings, etc, or based on a max amount of concurrent connections.

Next, we declare the servers in the *application.properties*:

```
commentstore.ribbon.eureka.enabled=false
commentstore.ribbon.listOfServers=localhost:8001,boiling-
retreat-23464.herokuapp.com:443
```

The configuration of our Ribbon client is always prefixed by its name, here *commentstore. ribbon.eureka.enabled* disables any service discovery in the Ribbon client as we are not yet implementing this step. And *ribbon.listOfServers* contains a comma-separated list of servers and their port.

So far, we have configured the client-side load balancer and it is now available in the Spring ApplicationContext. However, no instance of a *RestTemplate* is using it yet.

To use it, we must first add the *@LoadBalanced* annotation to the *restTemplate* method in *ConsumerApplication*. This will mark our *RestTemplate* as load balanced and the class is now proxied by Spring Clouds Ribbon client.

```
@Bean
@LoadBalanced
RestTemplate restTemplate(
  @Value("${commentstore.auth.user}")
  String username,
  @Value("${commentstore.auth.password}")
  String password,
```

```
    RestTemplateBuilder restTemplateBuilder)
{
    RestTemplate restTemplate =
                            restTemplateBuilder.build();
    restTemplate.getInterceptors().add(
      0,
      new BasicAuthorizationInterceptor(
        username,
        password
      )
    );
    return restTemplate;
}
```

We must define in *CommentService* that we want to receive a load balanced *RestTemplate* by also adding the *@LoadBalanced* annotation to the *restTemplate* attribute.

```
@Autowired
@LoadBalanced
private RestTemplate restTemplate;
```

Regular *RestTemplate* and load balanced one can co-exist in a Spring Context. With the *@LoadBalanced* annotation you request a load balanced one and leaving it out will assign a regular one.

What's left is to switch the endpoint from a real URL to the one using the name of the Ribbon client. So, the *endpoint* attribute in *CommentService* is set fixed to the URL using the Ribbons client's name (plus I made it static).

```
private static final String ENDPOINT = "https://
commentstore";
```

If you run the commentstore locally, change the URL to *http://commentstore*.

When you start the consumer application now and make your first request, you'll notice in the logs that the Ribbon client will now also try to access *localhost:8001* which will, of course, fail, because we haven't deployed any application there. But it's a good test to see the Ribbon client in action.

Our previously added retry mechanism is still in use and combined with the Ribbon client makes our application much more reliable than before.

Conclusion

In this version, we introduced the strategy called client-side load balancing and the possibility to add new microservice instance without having a central server-based load balancer in action. The client will determine by itself, which server of a list of service instance it will use.

In the simplest variant, the client does simply go through the list and pick the next server for a request. However, it would only detect an offline server after it tried to connect to it. We can enhance this by adding a regular ping which checks if the service is available in general and keeping track of unresponsive servers.

In cases that no service was available at all, we fall back to the retry mechanism from the previous chapter.

This approach works and is simple to implement. However, it also does have some drawbacks. First, each time we provide a new instance of a service, we must update the configuration of the client. Depending on your context, it might force a redeployment of the application, or a short application reload.

The other thing is, that we can only use the fallback after the Ribbon client made a request. When the commentstore service went down, it would still try to connect to it on each request and only after doing so we will enter the fallback path. On low traffic applications this might be ok but when you have hundreds of requests and all fail on the same path it will slow down your application, too. Wouldn't it be great to enter directly into the fallback path when we knew the service is down? Luckily, that's exactly what the circuit breaker pattern is for and we will introduce it in the next chapter.

Recap

Before we move on to the next variant, let's check your understanding with some open-ended questions:

- How do you configure a load-balanced RestTemplate?

- Can Spring Retry and the load balanced RestTemplate be used together?

- What is RoundRobin?

- What will happen when no microservice is available?

Circuit Breaker

In this chapter, we are going to make our client more intelligent in detecting service outages by introducing the circuit breaker pattern.

The solution from the previous chapter has one problem. It only uses the fallback path after actually trying to connect to any of the service instances behind the Ribbon client. If all instances of the service are down or have load issues, the Ribbon client will still try to connect them on each request before giving up and our retry mechanism will take over. In high load applications, this puts enormous pressure on the consumer application too. It would be much easier and faster to directly use the fallback if we detect issues with the subsequent services. That's exactly what a circuit breaker does. It uses heuristics to detect service outages and sends all following requests to the same services directly into the fallback path. After a certain period, it will send occasional requests to the services again to see if they are still unresponsive and after a grace period, it will activate the route again.

To implement the circuit breaker pattern we will use Spring Cloud with Hystrix, also part of Netflix OSS and a ready-to-use implementation for the pattern. Our new solution will also replace the previous mechanism using Spring Retry.

You can find the working sample in the branch *consumer-clb-circuitbreaker*.

To get started, add the following dependency to the pom:

```
<dependency>
    <groupId>org.springframework.cloud</groupId>
```

```
<artifactId>spring-cloud-starter-hystrix</artifactId>
</dependency>
```

Next, we add the *@EnableCircuitBreaker* annotation to *Consumer-Application* to enable a circuit breaker. This will set up Hystrix for us and we can start to use it with a single annotation in the next step. In the same attempt, we can remove the Spring Retry annotations in *CommentService* and *ConsumerApplication* as we are not using it anymore.

```
@SpringBootApplication
@EnableCircuitBreaker
@RibbonClient(
  name = "commentstore",
  configuration = RibbonConfig.class
)
public class ConsumerApplication {
    //omitted code
}
```

To use Hystrix now, Spring Cloud provides a single annotation *@HystrixCommand* which marks a method to be proxied by Hystrix.

```
@HystrixCommand(fallbackMethod = "recover")
public CommentDTO[] getComments(String productId) {
    LOGGER.info("requesting comments for product {}",
            productId);
    CommentDTO[] response = restTemplate.getForObject(
            ENDPOINT + "/list/" + productId,
            new CommentDTO[0].getClass()
    );

    return response;
}
```

Hystrix does three things here. First, it will keep track of failed executions; our method exits with a *Exception*. Second, on a failure, it will execute a fallback method (*fallbackMethod*) and third, if the failure rate rises above a threshold it won't execute our *getComments* method, but rather the fallback method.

The fallback method should have the same signature as the Hystrix proxied one and must also reside in the same class. It behaves similarly to the Spring Retry way. How you handle the failure depends on your context. For the example application, we return an empty list like in the retry solution before.

```
public CommentDTO[] recover(String productId) {
    LOGGER.info("requesting comments for product {}
failed, Hystrix aborted", productId);
    return new CommentDTO[0];
}
```

As an exercise, you can transform the *postComment* method to using Hystrix. You can find a working solution in the examples' branch.

Timeouts

When you use Hystrix commands that wrap Ribbon clients, as in the example above, you want to make sure to configure the timeout for Hystrix longer than the timeout of a Ribbon client. The timeout of the Ribbon client includes connection timeouts and all times of potential retries that might be made. For example, if your Ribbon connection timeout is three seconds and the Ribbon client retries the request three times, then your Hystrix timeout should be slightly more than nine seconds.

The timeouts are configured in the *application.properties* like:

```
hystrix.command.default.execution.isolation.thread.timeou
tInMilliseconds=10000
ribbon.ConnectTimeout=3000
ribbon.ReadTimeout=1000
```

When the *ribbon.** properties are not prefixed with the Ribbon clients name they are defaults for all Ribbon clients in the same application.

Hystrix Dashboard

Hystrix provides a small dashboard application for displaying all
@HystrixCommand annotated methods in an application with their
stats. It also shows if a gate is open aka the service is not reachable
and thus Hystrix directly executes the fallback.

```
<dependency>
    <groupId>org.springframework.cloud</groupId>
    <artifactId>spring-cloud-starter-hystrix-dashboard
    </artifactId>
</dependency>
```

Add the *@EnableHystrixDashboard* annotation to *ConsumerApplica-*
tion for enabling the Hystrix dashboard.

```
@SpringBootApplication
@EnableCircuitBreaker
@EnableHystrixDashboard
@RibbonClient(
  name = "commentstore",
  configuration = RibbonConfig.class
)
public class ConsumerApplication {
```

```
        //omitted code
    }
```

An application using Hystrix can make the state of the Hystrix data available as a stream. For a Spring Boot application, we only need to add the Spring Boot actuators to the pom to enabled it. This will make the endpoint *hystrix.stream* available under the actuator management (defaults to */application* in Spring Boot 2); so the stream is available under */application/hystrix.stream*.

When you start the application with the dashboard it is accessible under the path */hystrix* and you can point your browser to it.

Testing

In this section, we are going to put some load on the application to show off Hystrix. Reduce the Hystrix timeout above to one second, start the application and open the Hystrix dashboard.

Open a terminal. We are using the Apache HTTP server benchmarking tool which is part of the Apache HTTPD distribution. If you are on MacOS or *unix you probably already have it on your machine.

```
ab -n 30 -c 5 localhost:8080/
```

This will start the tool and send 30 requests in 5 concurrent threads to the given URL, our product details page. You should get some stats in the Hystrix dashboard but the command probably won't fail. Now stop the commentstore instances and run *ab* again.

It should fail now and the *Circuit* field should state *Open* in red now. As long as the circuit is open, Hystrix will execute our fallback method and at some point start to evaluate the connection again and eventually closing the circuit. Thus it routes to the microservice again.

Conclusion

In this version, we replaced our simple retry mechanism using Spring Retry with Hystrix, an implementation of the circuit breaker pattern. It looks similar at first, but there are differences.

What both solutions have in common is that we have some kind of fallback mechanism when a request fails. But the differences show up when we take a look at the trigger of the fallback in each solution.

When using simple retries, the fallback is triggered after a set of requests to the service were made (or at least tried) and they all failed. We actually have to make the calls.

With the circuit breaker, this is different as the fallback is called on an acute error or when the heuristics detect a service downtime and thus prevent making requests at all. This allows it to route calls based on previous experiences and to isolate the service so it can heal itself (or become restarted). In addition, it will prevent a slowdown in the consumer application due to unresponsive backends.

The pattern is highly usable on high load applications where parts can still continue to work properly even a single service is dead.

Handling this scenario is the job of the circuit breaker and Hystrix does do a fine job. However, something like retries isn't part of the pattern and so it does not exist. You can, of course, use Spring Retry for this and combine both techniques. However, be aware that both work with proxies in Spring and thus are only applicable when called from outside the proxy. The annotations won't work when used on private methods or methods called in the same class (You could use AspectJ during compile time for archiving that though).

Yet, all solutions we've implemented until now do not help in adding a single service instance on demand without any configuration and potential restarts. In the next chapter, we are going to use a service registry to finally solve this problem.

Recap

Before we move on to the next variant, let's check your understanding with some open-ended questions:

* What does a circuit breaker do?

* How can you configure Hystrix in Spring Boot?

* What annotation do you use for wrapping a method with Hystrix?

* Does Hystrix do retries?

Service Discovery

The previous solutions made our application more fault tolerant but we still had to manually add a new service instance in each consuming application and maybe even in redeploying them. This is definitely a problem when you need to quickly scale some services. Luckily, there's also a common pattern available for it: a service registry.

You can find the working sample in the branch *consumer-clb-cb-registry*.

We continue to use Spring Cloud for this and use the Netflix Eureka service registry.

The service registry will run as a separate Spring Boot application. Therefore, create a new Maven module and also add it as a module to the Maven parent project:

```
<project
  xmlns="http://maven.apache.org/POM/4.0.0"
  xmlns:xsi="http://www.w3.org/2001/XMLSchema-instance"
  xsi:schemaLocation="http://maven.apache.org/POM/4.0.0
    http://maven.apache.org/xsd/maven-4.0.0.xsd">
  <modelVersion>4.0.0</modelVersion>
  <parent>
    <groupId>org.springframework.boot</groupId>
    <artifactId>spring-boot-starter-parent</artifactId>
    <version>2.0.0.M2</version>
  </parent>
  <groupId>de.codeboje.springbootbook</groupId>
  <version>1.0.0-SNAPSHOT</version>
  <artifactId>registry</artifactId>
  <name>Spring Boot Intermediate Microservice Book -
Registry App</name>
```

```xml
<dependencies>
  <dependency>
    <groupId>org.springframework.cloud</groupId>
    <artifactId>spring-cloud-starter-eureka-server</artifactId>
  </dependency>
  <dependency>
    <groupId>org.springframework.cloud</groupId>
    <artifactId>spring-cloud-starter-config</artifactId>
  </dependency>
  <dependency>
    <groupId>org.springframework.boot</groupId>
    <artifactId>spring-boot-devtools</artifactId>
    <optional>true</optional>
  </dependency>
</dependencies>
</project>
```

Eureka is provided in the *spring-cloud-starter-eureka-server* module.

Next, create the *@SpringBootApplication* for it and add the *@EnableEurekaServer* annotation like:

```java
@SpringBootApplication
@EnableEurekaServer
public class RegistryApplication {
    public static void main(String[] args) {
        new SpringApplicationBuilder(
          RegistryApplication.class
          )
          .web(WebApplicationType.SERVLET)
          .run(args);
    }
}
```

@EnableEurekaServer will auto configure the application to start with a Eureka service. However, we still need to configure a few things in the *application.properties*:

```
spring.application.name=registry

server.port=8761

eureka.instance.hostname=localhost
eureka.client.registerWithEureka=false
eureka.client.fetchRegistry=false
eureka.client.serviceUrl.defaultZone=http://$
{eureka.instance.hostname}:${server.port}/eureka/
```

- *spring.application.name*: defines a name for the application, i.e. is used as an ID in the service registry and in later chapters.

- *server.port*: defines the port our registry listens on

- *eureka.instance.hostname*: defines the hostname of this Eureka instance

- *eureka.client.registerWithEureka*: Disable registering itself as a client

- *eureka.client.fetchRegistry*: Disable registering itself as a client

- *eureka.client.serviceUrl.defaultZone*: points to the default instance of a Eureka service; here our local instance

You could run multiple instances of a Eureka service and enable self-registration of Eureka. However, we use the standalone mode and thus disable the Eureka client with the *eureka.client.* properties above.

You can start the registry now and access it with a browser on *http://localhost:8761/eureka* to see a list of registered services and instances. However, right now it will still be empty as we haven't configured the commentstore and consumer yet.

Registering the Commentstore

To enabled the Eureka client we must add its dependency to the pom:

```
<dependency>
  <groupId>org.springframework.cloud</groupId>
  <artifactId>spring-cloud-starter-eureka</artifactId>
</dependency>
```

Next, we enable the service discovery by adding the *@EnableDiscoveryClient* annotation to the configuration class:

```
@EnableDiscoveryClient
public class CommentStoreApp {
    //omitted code and other annotations
}
```

This will enable the discovery client and register our application with the registry. In *application.properties* we set an ID for our service and point to the Eureka server instance like:

```
spring.application.name=commentstore
eureka.client.serviceUrl.defaultZone=http://localhost:
8761/eureka/
```

When you start the commentstore now, you'll notice in the log files that it tries to register itself on the service registry. When finished you can see the service in the Eureka UI on *http://localhost: 8761/eureka*. Note that it might take a while for first registration.

Registering the Consumer

As with the commentstore before, add the dependency to your pom and enable the discovery client with the *@EnableDiscovery-Client* annotation on *ConsumerApplication*.

Now we can configure it in the *application.properties*.

Starting with this example you cannot use my Heroku instance of the commentstore service but you will need to run it locally now. Therefore we switch its port to *8081* and also give it an identifier.

```
spring.application.name=consumer
server.port=8081
eureka.client.serviceUrl.defaultZone=http://localhost:
8761/eureka/

commentstore.ribbon.eureka.enabled=true
```

We point the Eureka client also to our registry using *eureka.client.-serviceUrl.defaultZone* and finally enable the service discovery for our Ribbon client named *commentstore* with *commentstore.ribbon.eu-reka.enabled*.

When you start the consumer application now, it will also try to register at the registry, but it will also use the registry to find any instances of a service with the same name as our Ribbon client (*commentstore*).

When all applications are running you can access the consumer again and it should route all requests to the commentstore URL now to your commentstore instance.

Conclusion

Adding a service registry to our application makes it possible to add a new instance of the commentstore service just by starting them. We do not need to configure a new instance on each deploy artifact of the consumer application. A new commentstore will auto-register itself in the service registry and the consuming applications can find it there.

The service registry contract with Eureka requires each service to send a heartbeat every 30s. If the heartbeat fails, the service instance is not available anymore. However, this is not immediately effective on a client due to the fact that the Eureka server and the client keep a separate cache for a default of 30s. So if a service fails, it propagates with a delay of 90s to the clients. You can, of course, adjust those times in the configuration if necessary. However, this depends highly on your scenario.

The huge benefit of the registry is that we can add or remove services at will, without the need to propagate it with any configuration changes. When we combine this with Cloud deployments we can set up a new service instance in probably a few minutes.

Client-side load balancing combined with the service registry is a pretty smooth solution for making an application more reliable. However, it also exposes a problem if you want to allow access to your service from outside of your department or company. Giving externals access to your service registry and individual services is not a good idea in regard to security and also puts a lot of implementation load on the client side. However, we can continue to use the client-side load balancing and service registry internally and add a gateway in front of them for external access. In the next chapter, we will cover one solution for this.

Recap

Before we move on to the next variant, let's check your understanding with some open-ended questions.

- How do you create a Service Registry Server?

- How to register the commentstore service with the registry?

- How can you configure the Ribbon clients to find the service instances in the service registry?

Moving behind a Gateway

When we build applications in a microservice (or service oriented architecture) we will sooner or later face the problem that we need to expose all or certain aspects in an API for use by third parties. It doesn't matter if they are in-house or external, you usually do not want them to deal with your infrastructure for many reasons.

The traditional way of doing this is to put your services behind a proxy and let all clients only communicate with the proxy. How your services are setup doesn't matter for the client anymore. The only thing the client needs to know is the new endpoints of the services on the proxy. However, classical proxies have a more static configuration and don't use a service registry for discovering available services.

A solution to this problem is to use Netflix Zuul. Zuul is a proxy which supports service discovery, circuit breaker, client-side load balancing and more. We'll use it with Spring Cloud and as a simple gateway aka proxy for our consumer application and commentstore.

You can find the working sample in the branch *consumer-clb-cb-registry-gateway*.

Let's get our hands dirty and build a simple gateway. The gateway will run as a separate Spring Boot application. Therefore, let's create a new Maven module and also add it as a module to the Maven parent project:

```
<project
  xmlns="http://maven.apache.org/POM/4.0.0"
  xmlns:xsi="http://www.w3.org/2001/XMLSchema-instance"
  xsi:schemaLocation="http://maven.apache.org/POM/4.0.0
```

```
        http://maven.apache.org/xsd/maven-4.0.0.xsd">
    <modelVersion>4.0.0</modelVersion>
    <parent>
        <groupId>org.springframework.boot</groupId>
        <artifactId>spring-boot-starter-parent</artifactId>
        <version>2.0.0.M2</version>
    </parent>
    <groupId>de.codeboje.springbootbook</groupId>
    <version>1.0.0-SNAPSHOT</version>
    <artifactId>gateway</artifactId>
    <name>Spring Boot Intermediate Microservice Book -
Gateway App</name>

    <dependencies>
        <dependency>
            <groupId>org.springframework.cloud</groupId>
            <artifactId>spring-cloud-starter-zuul</artifactId>
        </dependency>
        <dependency>
            <groupId>org.springframework.cloud</groupId>
            <artifactId>spring-cloud-starter-eureka</
artifactId>
        </dependency>
        <dependency>
            <groupId>org.springframework.boot</groupId>
            <artifactId>spring-boot-devtools</artifactId>
            <optional>true</optional>
        </dependency>
    </dependencies>
</project>
```

The gateway is provided by the *spring-cloud-starter-zuul* starter and
we use Eureka for discovering service instances.

Next, create the *@SpringBootApplication* for it and add the
@EnableZuulProxy annotation for enabling the Zuul proxy and
@EnableDiscoveryClient for using the service registry like:

```
@SpringBootApplication
@EnableDiscoveryClient
```

```
@EnableZuulProxy
public class GatewayApplication {
    public static void main(String[] args) {
        new SpringApplicationBuilder(
          GatewayApplication.class
        )
        .web(WebApplicationType.SERVLET)
        .run(args);
    }
}
```

@EnableZuulProxy will autoconfigure the application to start with a Zuul proxy. However, we still need to configure a few things in the *application.properties*:

```
spring.application.name=gateway
server.port=8082

eureka.client.serviceUrl.defaultZone=http://localhost:
8761/eureka/

zuul.sensitiveHeaders=

zuul.routes.commentstore=/api/**

zuul.routes.ui.path=/**
zuul.routes.ui.url=http://localhost:8081/
```

As we are testing all local, we assign a separate port to the gateway and also give it an identifier for the service registry. We will also use service discovery and point to our Eureka instance.

Our simple gateway will only handle two paths.

1. */api* : the public path for our commentstore API

2. */***: and the rest will point to the consumer application

Routes are added under the prefix *zuul.routes* and can follow two schemas. A simple one with direct service name to route mapping and a more configurable one. We use the simple one for routing the commentstore API, so let's take a look at the configuration.

```
zuul.routes.commentstore=/api/**
```

Here we declare a route for a service named *commentstore* to be available under */api/*. What happens now is when Zuul receives a request to */api/list/product4711* it will forward the wildcard part to a service instance of the service named *commentstore*. It uses Eureka to look up the service instances and forwards the request to */list/product4711* on the service instance. When you fire the request now using Postman, our gateway will forward it to an available service instance. However, it will fail because by default Zuul isn't forwarding certain sensitive headers like the *Authorization* header. With the *zuul.sensitiveHeaders* property we can override the sensitive headers and define none, so all headers router through.

The other routing configuration behaves a bit different. The name we use after the *zuul.routes.* prefix is just a simple identifier.

```
zuul.routes.ui.path=/**
zuul.routes.ui.url=http://localhost:8081/
```

With *path* we define the route and map everything at */*** to be forwarded to the URL we define in the next line with *url*. Instead of the *url*, we could also use *serviceId* to define a mapping to a particular service. However, the difference to the simple notation before is that the value defined in *path* is forwarded to the service as is. So, if we would route from */api/*** to our commentstore using this format, Zuul will also forward to */api/* on our microservice (which is running under the root path).

We could also define other properties like the *sensitiveHeaders* on each route individually by just defining them under the service prefix.

Hint: Routes should usually not intersect, or if they do, you must specify them in order. However, the order might not be preserved when using property files but they are when you use the YAML configuration. In this simple example, it always worked with the property file.

Before we can start all applications and access the consumer and commentstore via the proxy, we must make the consumer aware of being behind a proxy by adding a single property in the *application.properties* of the consumer:

```
server.use-forward-headers=true
```

This will make Spring MVC aware that it is behind a proxy and respect the *X-FORWARD-** headers accordingly (especially after the redirect after a new comment was posted).

Start the registry, commentstore, consumer and gateway now and then you can send requests using Postman to the new */api* endpoint or access the UI via the proxy using *http://localhost:8082/*.

Conclusion

A gateway or proxy is commonly used in applications and does a great job in providing central access points and hiding infrastructure or even handling SSL and security. The jobs a proxy can handle are manifold. With a microservice orientated architecture, I think they are even more important and especially must make use of the patterns involved like service discovery, etc.

With the gateway, we could continue to use our solutions from before to make the application more reliable and at the same time, we make it much easier for future clients to communicate with our service. In the sample, we do only have one microservice but in practice, you will have dozens more. You can use common microservice patterns internally and provide a classic central entry point for external parties.

As a proxy like Zuul is easy to set up, it often makes sense to provide a specific API for a single client and just expose the microservices in use. For example, you could offer a separate gateway for your mobile client which only exposes the services in a way which is more suitable for your mobile client.

However, you need to be able to maintain your whole application landscape; be it financially, with knowledge or human power. I can't throw humans or money at you, but in the next chapter we are adding a central configuration store and make configuration a bit easier.

Recap

Before we move on to the next variant, let's check your understanding with some open-ended questions:

- What does a gateway do?

- How do you set up Zuul with Spring Cloud?

- Can you keep the routes in order?

Centralize Configuration

In this last practical chapter, we are moving the configuration of our applications to a centralized configuration store.

When we have many services deployed it can become cumbersome with keeping the configuration of each service in sync. Often a simple configuration change requires a new release and deployment of the service to all of its instances. Depending on your context, this might be no problem at all, but often it is not that easy to distribute configuration changes.

However, when we add a central place for the configuration it becomes much easier and also reduces the setup time of new service instances. For setting up a central configuration storage we will use Spring Cloud Config which provides out-of-the-box functionality for this task.

You can find the working sample in the branch *consumer-clb-cb-registry-gateway-config*.

The config store will run as a separate Spring Boot application. Therefore, create a new Maven module and also add it as a module to the Maven parent project:

```
<project
  xmlns="http://maven.apache.org/POM/4.0.0"
  xmlns:xsi="http://www.w3.org/2001/XMLSchema-instance"
  xsi:schemaLocation="http://maven.apache.org/POM/4.0.0
    http://maven.apache.org/xsd/maven-4.0.0.xsd">
  <modelVersion>4.0.0</modelVersion>
  <parent>
    <groupId>org.springframework.boot</groupId>
    <artifactId>spring-boot-starter-parent</artifactId>
    <version>2.0.0.M2</version>
```

```
    </parent>
    <groupId>de.codeboje.springbootbook</groupId>
    <version>1.0.0-SNAPSHOT</version>
    <artifactId>config</artifactId>
    <name>Spring Boot Intermediate Microservice Book -
Configuration App</name>

    <dependencies>
      <dependency>
        <groupId>org.springframework.cloud</groupId>
        <artifactId>spring-cloud-config-server</artifactId>
      </dependency>
      <dependency>
        <groupId>org.springframework.boot</groupId>
        <artifactId>spring-boot-devtools</artifactId>
        <optional>true</optional>
      </dependency>
    </dependencies>
  </project>
```

The config store is provided by the *spring-cloud-config-server* starter and we will also create a *@SpringBootApplication* for it. Add the *@EnableConfigServer* annotation for enabling the configuration server like:

```
@SpringBootApplication
@EnableConfigServer
public class ConfigApplication {
    public static void main(String[] args) {
        new SpringApplicationBuilder(
          ConfigApplication.class
        )
        .run(args);
    }
}
```

Next, we will give it (like the other components) a unique identifier and define a port of the config server.

```
spring.application.name=config
server.port=8888

spring.cloud.config.server.native.search-
locations=classpath:/shared
spring.profiles.active=native
```

Spring Cloud Config can store the configuration using multiple backends, e.g. Git, file, vault, etc. For the example, we are using the file-based backend and can lookup the config files in the classpath. We enable the file backend by setting the property *spring.profiles.active* to *native*. And with the property *spring.cloud.config.server.native.search-locations* we define where the config server will look up the configuration of the services.

As with any Spring Boot application, we can use either property or YAML files. There are two different config files for the services. First, an *application.properties* which will be used for all services, and second, one for a particular service with the service name as the base file name.

Let's start with the common one and create a *application.properties* under *src/main/resources/shared* in the config project.

```
eureka.client.serviceUrl.defaultZone=http://localhost:
8761/eureka/
```

In this, we only point all clients to the Eureka server so they can register and find services.

Next, we are creating a *commentstore.properties* to hold the configuration of our commentstore service. The identifier in use is the name of the service we set earlier with *spring.application.name* in the property file of the service.

```
sbb.spamwords.filename=/words.spam

# local h2 in-memory db
spring.datasource.url=jdbc:h2:mem:mydb
spring.datasource.username=sa

spring.jpa.hibernate.ddl-auto=update

# jpa validation query
spring.datasource.test-on-borrow=true
spring.datasource.validation-query=SELECT 1

security.user.name=admin
security.user.password=mypassword
```

If a commentstore service instance would now request its configuration, it will receive a joined version of the *application.properties* and *commentstore.properties* from the *shared* folder.

In the commentstore, we must implement two things. First, we must enable the cloud configuration by adding the *spring-cloud-starter-config* to the pom:

```
<dependency>
  <groupId>org.springframework.cloud</groupId>
  <artifactId>spring-cloud-starter-config</artifactId>
</dependency>
```

Second, we replace the *application.properties* with a *bootstrap.properties* file and only keep some tiny essentials config:

```
spring.application.name=commentstore
spring.cloud.config.uri=http://localhost:8888
spring.cloud.config.failFast=true
```

The injection of the properties with the values provided by the config server must happen before any of the regular config processing in Spring Boot starts. This can be archived by using a *boot-*

strap.properties file. This is scanned and handled by Spring Cloud Config to locate the actual configuration.

In it we define the name of our service which is also used for getting the correct configuration, point it to the config server *spring.cloud.config.uri* and define it should fail during startup if the config server is not available *spring.cloud.config.failFast*.

During startup, the config client will now try to connect to the config server and load its configuration. If the config server is not online, the startup will fail. When we add Spring Retry and the AOP starter to our pom, Spring Cloud Config will automatically retry 6 times with an exponential backoff policy to connect to the config server.

You can switch the gateway, registry, and consumer now also to use the config server by following the same steps as above.

When you are ready, start the config server, service registry, gateway, commentstore, and consumer application. Check if anything runs again.

Conclusion

A central configuration server takes the config burden away from the clients. This makes the deployment of a new instance of a single service easier and also the propagation of new configuration values.

In the example, we used a simple file based configuration store but in your projects, you can also use a version control system like Git for storing the configurations. This has the huge benefit of having an audit log automatically so you can see who made the changes, and where and when.

You can work with a single config server as it's only needed during startup of the applications. However, depending on your context it might be preferable to run either two instances behind a proxy or by using it like any other service and registering it with a service registry. In the later case, the client would need to know the URL of the service registry. For example, if you dynamically add and remove service instances based on traffic, you have the need of a higher availability and should probably run two or more instances of the config server. On the contrary, if you only distribute occasional changes, it might not be worth to add more instances.

Recap

Before we move on to the next variant, let's check your understanding with some open-ended questions:

* How do I set up the config server?

* How do you configure a client to use the config server?

* Does the client still use a application.properties file?

Conclusion

In the book you have learned some solutions for working with microservices and how to implement them for your Spring Boot applications. They are all proven solutions and libraries and work. However, as tempting it might be for some developers, not every solution works for every problem.

It depends.

One might be tempted to dismiss the first retry solution because it doesn't improve the application much in regards of reliability. That might be true for certain complex scenarios. However, it might still work and be the preferred solution for smaller scale applications.

It might also be a good step for moving from a monolithic application to a more service-oriented architecture. Not everyone has the time, money, and staff to build a full scale microservice architecture.

Also, the solutions here are also not limited to a microservice architecture. You can use part of them with regular applications like the gateway, circuit breaker or a central configuration. They might help you in solving a particular problem in your context.

Depending on your application it might also work to just start with the basic version we used first. It has its flaws but it might be better to start with a prototype fast and gain experience. You can always add the more complex solutions later when your baby, or your customers' baby flies.

At the end of the day we are developing applications for solving a business need and not just for the sake of developing it. So, when you apply these solutions to an actual problem, keep it mind that it must make sense in this concrete context. If your customer publishes a public API like Twitter or Contentful, they can't go with the simple solution. They need to run a full fledged version. Otherwise, they might go out of business pretty soon.

On the contrary, when they build a simple CRUD app for in-house use or a directory site, it's overkill to go with the full fledge version. They might go bankrupt before you even deliver the application. Sometimes, even the simple version is enough. And their need grows, you can still extend the application and introduce one of the other solutions.

Thank You

Thank you for taking time and following along. I hope I could help you to level up with Microservices in Spring Boot.

You can read more about Spring Boot on the resource page (http://codeboje.de/sbb3-resources/) of the book and I encourage you to also connect with me. Honestly, if you have further questions, or just want advice on how to continue now, do not hesitate and reach out. I am glad to help out.

You can either reach me via my blog codeboje.de or directly via the exclusive email address book@codeboje.de .

Happy coding

Jens

Appendix A: Using Spring Boot 2 Milestones

We use Milestone 2 of the Spring Boot 2 in the book. However, as it is not a final release, it is not available in Maven Central. For using the Milestone version, we must add the Spring Milestone Maven repository to each of our project.

As we are building a few Spring Boot applications and it's a common task I'll include the dependency here once.

```
<repositories>
    <repository>
        <id>spring-milestones</id>
        <name>Spring Milestones</name>
        <url>https://repo.spring.io/libs-milestone</url>
        <snapshots>
            <enabled>false</enabled>
        </snapshots>
    </repository>
    <repository>
        <id>spring-snapshots</id>
        <name>Spring Snapshots</name>
        <url>https://repo.spring.io/libs-snapshot</url>
        <snapshots>
            <enabled>true</enabled>
        </snapshots>
    </repository>
</repositories>

// continues on next page
```

```xml
<pluginRepositories>
    <pluginRepository>
        <id>spring-milestones</id>
        <name>Spring Milestones</name>
        <url>https://repo.spring.io/libs-milestone</url>
        <snapshots>
            <enabled>false</enabled>
        </snapshots>
    </pluginRepository>
</pluginRepositories>
```

Appendix B: Deploy to Heroku

Deploying a Spring Boot application is straight forward. Heroku offers two ways of deploying applications. First, using a Git repository and pushing the source code. Heroku will then build the application in their infrastructure and finally deploy the build artifact. Second, we can do a binary deploy using the Maven Heroku Plugin. It does build the application locally and deploys only the build artifacts to Heroku.

Step 1

Install the Heroku CLI. You can download it here (https://dev-center.heroku.com/articles/heroku-cli#download-and-install)

Step 2

Create an account on Heroku (https://signup.heroku.com/).

Step 3

Open a terminal window and change into the directory of the sample application. For the deployment, the application must be inside a git repository.

And then we can log in the first time

```
heroku login
```

Step 4

Now, we can create our *commentstore* application and link it:

```
heroku create <app-name>
```

This will create a git repository on Heroku for the *commentstore* application and link it as a remote in our repository under the name *heroku*. The app name is optional and if you do not specify one, Heroku generates one.

Step 5

Create the Postgres service:

```
heroku addons:create heroku-postgresql:hobby-dev
```

It creates a Postgres service with the free hobby-dev tier.

Step 6

Next, we need to declare in the *application.properties* which database to use:

```
spring.datasource.url=${JDBC_DATABASE_URL}
```

The environment variable *JDBC_DATABASE_URL* is provided by Heroku and contains the full JDBC string for connecting to the database.

Step 7a - Git Deploy

Next, we must define for Heroku what type of application we have and how to start it.

Create a file named *Procfile* in the root of the git repository.

```
web: java -Dserver.port=$PORT -jar comment-store/target/
sbb-comment-app.jar
```

It defines a web dyno running the java command and we specify the jar file to run and set the port used by Heroku.

In simple cases, i.e. we only have one maven project in the git repository, Heroku automatically determines what to run.

Now we are ready for deploying our application for the first time.

Your changes have to be committed.

```
git push heroku master
```

This will push our master branch to Heroku. Heroku will now build our application, creating some artifacts for further rollout and finally deploys it to their infrastructure.

Step 7b - Deploy using the Heroku Maven Plugin

The git deploy variant forces you to push your source code to Heroku. It's not the best way for everyone. As an alternative, Heroku provides a way for binary deployments and offers a Maven plugin for the Java world .

Add the plugin to the plugins section in your pom.

```
<plugin>
    <groupId>com.heroku.sdk</groupId>
    <artifactId>heroku-maven-plugin</artifactId>
    <version>1.1.3</version>
    <configuration>
        <processTypes>
            <web>java $JAVA_OPTS -Dserver.port=$PORT -cp
                target/classes:target/dependency/*
                de.codeboje.springbootbook.
                      commentstore.CommentStoreApp
            </web>
        </processTypes>
    </configuration>
</plugin>
```

Next, we need to configure the type of the application and what to run using the *processTypes* parameter. The difference to our *Procfile* version is that we do not specify the final jar file here, but rather add two directories. The first is *target/classes* which contains our compiled application classes (regular Maven folder) and second, *target/dependency/* which contains all dependencies of our application and is created by the Heroku plugin.

The Heroku plugin will use the app name in the git repository. If your project is not in a git repo, you must specify the application name in the configuration above like:

```
<configuration>
    <appName>commentstore</appName>
</configuration>
```

However, we use git, so let's just deploy using Maven:

```
mvn clean heroku:deploy
```

This builds the application on your machine using Maven and then deploy the binary artifacts to Heroku.

Make a Request

When done you could access your application.

```
heroku open
```

This command opens your application in the browser. Call any of the actuators like *application/health* and you should get a valid response.

Use Postman and the collection (https://github.com/azarai/springbootbook/blob/with-spring-boot-2m/SpringBootBook.-postman_collection) and adjust the requests to the endpoint of your application.

Remove the App again

When you are done, you can remove the app again by running:

```
heroku apps:destroy <app-name>
```

You don't want to use free dyno time for a tutorial app, don't you?

Integrate it With a Single-Page Application

Learn 4 ways to integrate your Spring Boot application with a single-page application securely in the same actionable and hands-on approach.

http://codeboje.de/spring-boot-single-page-applications/